Tunes & Tens

Tunes & Tens

Kit Robinson

ROOF BOOKS
New York

ISBN: 979-8-9915011-3-2
Library of Congress Control Number: 2025931442

Cover art by Ericka McConnell
Author photo by Ahni Robinson
Book design by Deborah Thomas
Editor: James Sherry

Parts of this book have appeared in online and print publications, including *Broken Lens, The Café Review, Eternal Sections, Julebord, Kickstand*, and *R&R*. Many thanks to the editors.

Thanks also to Ted Pearson and Stephen Emerson for invaluable help with the manuscript.

NEW YORK STATE OF OPPORTUNITY. Council on the Arts This book is made possible, in part, by the New York State Council on the Arts with the support of the office of the Governor and the New York State Legislature.

Roof Books
are published by
Segue Foundation
300 Bowery FL 2
New York, NY 10012
seguefoundation.com

For book orders, please go to
Independent Publishers Group
IPGbook.com

In memory of Lyn Hejinian (1941–2024)

Contents

Introduction

On Kit Robinson's *Tunes & Tens*

KNOWN as one of the formative figures of the Bay Area Language poetry moment, Kit Robinson's later poetry is in my mind some of his best, and his latest addition *Tunes & Tens* is no exception. During his years employed in the burgeoning tech industry in the 80s and 90s, Robinson embedded his poetry in the interstices of his working day by writing on the job, a practice Michel de Certeau called "la perruque," the French term for a worker's own work disguised as work for his employer. At times, this involved sampling computer jargon and business-speak and torquing it toward contrary ends that released it from its productivist logic, while at the same time integrating references to business travel (airports, hotel lobbies) and his daily commute. Rather than situating his poetry outside the labor that dominates our day-to-day lives, confining it to solitary retreats freed from material concerns, Robinson situated his practice squarely inside *the machine*, what his colleague Robert Grenier called "the counting house," referring to his own job at a corporate law firm in the Bay Area at the time.

Now in retirement, references to Robinson's travels continue but the language of the workplace has given way to the rituals of his day-to-day life, which includes practicing and performing in Calle Ocho, an Afro-Cuban charanga band in which he plays the tres, an acoustic guitar with three doubled strings. It's only natural then that the first section of *Tunes & Tens* begins with a series of poems written "after" jazz titans like Henry Threadgill, Thelonious Monk, Don Cherry, Carla Bley, and Billie Holiday, as well as the great late, dear friend of the poet's, Lyn Hejinian, to whom the book is dedicated. As such, the improvisatory spirit of jazz, including quotation, pervades the book, from the playful dissonance of Monk's angular compositions, the rebellious blast of Cherry's pocket trumpet, Bley's wry sense of humor, and the melancholic croon of Holiday. But it's not only jazz greats that form Robinson's musical lexicon. Appropriately we find poems inspired by Cuban bands like Orquesta Aragon and Changüí de Guantánamo as well as African artists like Boubacar Traoré, Sona Jobarteh, and Thomas Mapfumo.

"Tunes" is followed by "Tens," a serial poem comprising 73 ten-line stanzas or decimas. It is here that we find the polyphonic structure of Robinson's poetry. At times, this polyverse manifests itself in lines that stand alone, seemingly unrelated to those that follow, as in "Tens" stanza LVII, where each line is a quotation culled from poets included in Drew Gardner's *Ingenious Pleasures: An Anthology of Punk, Trash and Camp in 20th Century Poetry:*

> I have been over-exposed all my life
> Dancing, like kosher ice water
> Imagine throwing away the avalanche so early in
>   the movie
> Opprobrious shrilling
> Time, progress and good sense

Other times, the lines enjamb across two or more lines then shift to something different, in this case the "Heavy overhead" of the "atmospheric bomb" that hung over the Bay Area in January 2023:

> What's going on
> Is walking and talking
> By dint of foot and word of mouth
> 82 percent of Americans don't go nowhere
> The trees go wild in the wind
> The clouds open up into a downpour (VI)

Then there are the stanzas that stray from the paratactic to the kind of hypotaxis we find in conventional poetry, where one line flows into the next across the entire breadth of the stanza. Here we find what might be called "closed texts" in an otherwise open-text series, as in the case of the tenth stanza of "Tens" that describes the build-up to a musical performance:

> Music is all about scheduling
> Charged up on anticipation
> The host musician prepares the way
> Plugs in the devices
> Makes sure everything works

Or, take stanza XXXIII, which riffs off of Descartes' famous dictum "I think therefore I am," adding "I think therefore of others". . . "Including plants, animals, rivers, and mountains," a sentiment echoed later in stanza XLIV, with its nod to Whitman, "We are composite / Each one comprises multiple persons." Likewise, Robinson employs hypotaxis in stanza LXVI, an elegy devoted to the "memory of Susan Hopkins Coolidge," which captures perfectly the devastating sense of loss that pervades the book: "But how can one / So crucial to what's going on / Be so fully present / And then so suddenly not?"

Perhaps what's most notable, and risky, about Robinson's poetry is his use of flat language, a minimalist aesthetic utterly stripped of conventional poetic adornments. In "Song for My Father," such plain language is used to great effect, keeping the reader constantly off balance (and surprised), as it shifts from the sincere to the ironic and back to the sincere by way of cliché. Here's the beginning of the poem:

> Not all people have fathers
> There are lots of different ways to make a baby
> Many different ways to grow up
> Different people who can make a family
> My dad was always there for me

By the end of this autobiographical poem, which includes the following example of the poet's dry wit—"WWII / England / My mom / Evanston / Me"—Robinson doubles down on the cliché with the kind of affective punch that too often poets succumb to when dealing with weighty matters, but which, in this poet's masterful hands, strikes just the right tone, transforming a cliché into heart-felt sincerity: "He was always there, and he still is."

Tunes & Tens is a most timely work where the whole wide world is at play in the day-to-day, both the large and the small, macro and micro, the universe and a grain of sand, a world at war ("the fog of war") side by side with today's football game ("A tight end catches a long pass"), and "things to do on Mars," decontextualized language made strange and often humorous sometimes heart-breaking by its disjunctive surroundings. Like the newsfeeds constantly flashing across our screens, "365 keys / Times a hundred years of solitude," we find lines that often mimic the annoying intrusions of autocorrect, where the poet's daily thoughts must contend with prefab language, titles of novels, songs, movies that come to mind as they merge into the heavy traffic of clichés, colloquialisms, and platitudes. Robinson pushes his music—dare I say, his wisdom—through it all, time after time, always surprising, delighting, teaching, unlearning, rediscovering, dancing, mourning, riffing, and dying and somehow, above and below it all, carrying on. A new book by this prolific and most crucial of American poets is a gift that keeps on giving. *Tunes & Tens* will knock your socks off. Who could ask for anything more?

Tim Shaner
January 2025

Tunes

I CAN'T WAIT TO GET HOME

after Henry Threadgill

Don't pay me no nevermind
I'll be outta here soon

The war does not
Have my interest at heart

I was sent here
For sowing discord
In the national anthem
A true account
Of these disunited states

Eventually I made it back
To Chicago
To the sanctified church
Of my mother

THE LONDON COLLECTION

after Monk

Don't forget to tinkle
Before you get in the car
To go home
Words to the man
Who once was a boy

Then there he goes
The man I love
Spreading the word
Five fingers
On each of his hands

Maybe you remember
Him coming in late
Wearing his heart
On something blue
According to you

Introspection
Is not his strong suit
He'd rather be out
On the breezeway
Picking up speed

Perfectly balanced
On two big feet
Wide awake
When half asleep
Damn happy to be sad

What do you say
To someone with eyes
In the back of their head?
How's the weather
Back there?

Did you jig
When you shoulda jagged?
Where's the beat?
Are you still open?
Haven't I seen you someplace before?

This crepuscule
Is unlike any other
Out the window
Out on the street
Weather going away

Where did you get
That nutty idea?
The notes spill
Out of the chord
And onto the driveway

We discover nothing
Lest we explore
Be that as it may
It's good to be back
In Hackensack

WHERE IS BROOKLYN?

after Don Cherry

A conversation can go
In different directions
Depending on what?
The weather
Who's speaking
How does one feel
About what one is about to say?

Silence is burnt orange
A familial pause
In the rat-a-tat-tat
Of a trap set
A matter of hat
A chance to adjust
Depth of focus

The thing is
And is not an idea
In a procession of tenets
But an actual entity
In relation to other things
Too many to count
In one lifetime

Weaving in and out of traffic
The reckless driver
Adds risk to the equation
Of a Thursday afternoon
Something to tell about later

Over a light supper
Back home in the East Bay

There is the bomb
And then there is the shock
Felt all the way
To the Shake Shack
We tip-toe past the signs
Of life in the fast lane
And out to the beach at Far Rockaway

Watchers of the world, unite!
Time for a glimpse of what have you
The sweet center of a sour pop
That lasts as long as you do
Who have been here many times before
And always enjoy the situation
Of disbelief in boundaries

BEAUTIFUL TELEPHONES

after Carla Bley

I think to write freely
Like Spinoza
But not in Latin
Rather a desiccated English
Is my preferred medium
Bits of history
Cling to the underside of speech
A ray of hope in a glass tube

Military precision
Subjects the body to fits of rage
Hilarious birds flock to the marine band
A world of madcap humor
Lasts a definite while

A copycat like me
Enters a room
After you

What happens
Is entirely dependent
On what does not
Multiple outcomes
Get in each other's way

We hang out on the sidelines
And follow the action
On the lawns

The sun lights up the afternoon
These memories are marvelous
Even if patently false
Their particulars are pure invention
Composed as they are
Of disparate strands
A multi-colored fabric of delight
Whose imaginary future
Welcomes a continuing past

PIÈCES DE CLAVECIN

after François Couperin

A courtly gesture or phrase
Reflects the manner of the court
Formulaic passages
Winter spring summer fall
A wild savage from the Americas
An African bull
Spices from Siam, Sumbawa, Ceylon
Form the boundaries of custom
All strive to observe
In deference to the King

A country dance
What did one shepherdess's brother
Say to the other shepherdess's brother?
Let's get the flock outta here

AUBADE

after Lyn

I am concise
The world is prolix
Comprising as it does
The seven seas, a gram of cocaine, Jiminy Cricket,
    Transcendentalism
The horse you rode in on, flapjacks, pieces of eight,
    titanium rods
Ambergris, Alicia Keys, color field abstraction, a straight flush
Appendicitis, Monte Alban, Sugar Smacks, Santa Anita,
    cumulus clouds
Road maps, Don Quixote, a pair of pliers, flight simulators,
    Tenochtitlan
Grauman's Chinese Theatre, the Plymouth Hoe,
    California poppies, and trigonometry
In no particular order

Now let us inspect these apparitions in the light
    of day
But first the morning pills and morning news
Some tears well up as posts from friends of Lyn
    are read
But first a cup of coffee and a chat with Ahni
Full moon last night has been replaced by plucky sun
Ready for anything, to toast it with big love
Rivers of irritation undermine the arrangements
Condolences come pouring in
A swirl of bedclothes in the corner
A prelude to making the bed

MARIAMA KABA

after Boubacar Traoré

A heavy melancholy
Dogs my steps
From chicken-scratch yard
To desert trek

A lonely path
A sorry dance
From Bamako
To Paris, France

Always a visitor
Never at home
When I leave this place
Which way shall I go?

Is this all there is?
What can I say?
A rag to wipe
My tears away

The problem stems
From an ancient curse
To talk about it
Would only make it worse

Soon it will be time
For me to be on my way
We will see one another
Another day

STELLAR JAYS

after Neeli

I have my second cup of coffee
By the handle
One of many paths
To enlightenment
According to Hebraic bodhisattvas
At the Greyhound station
In San Bernadino in the 50s

On Red Mountain
Up at the summit
A dusting of snow
Campfire smoke my solitary
Inspiration when all else
Is set aside
To make room for an archive

How many nights and days
Are going to pass us by?
Dreams of Bob Kaufman
At the Trieste
Plenty of time for another cup
Or cross the street to City Lights
House of Ferlinghetti

You packed it all in
To your poems
With breathing space
Bad eyesight
Love of the greats

Infirmity, enthusiasm, style
Wild hairy brainchild moves

You skipped
Interiorly bound
Until discovering
The perfect cave
For living and dying
Plato was here
And Wim Wenders' smile

Sleeping off a film script
In the dawn
All rolled up
In a ball of light
One dimly espied
From across the yard
Where stellar jays make hay

I don't know how
To tell you this
As you are gone
From sight
But not from hearing
The thrum of the voice
Awake in the head

BADINYAA KUMOO

after Sona Jobarteh

She is a *griot*
Like her father before her
A singer of songs
A teller of tales of the tribe
A tribe called everyone
Within earshot
A shot in the dark called time

Tracks on a path
A voice in the night
Fingers on skins on fire
A matter of act
A boom chank in unfolding time

Sing me a lullaby
A lullaby for the child
I used to be
I will sing you a lullaby
A lullaby for the child
You used to be
A lullaby that stretches into pain

A riverbed people
Colonized for gain
Remember old stories
Songs' refrain
Waiting in darkness
For clouds to break open
For liberating rain

YOU DON'T KNOW WHAT LOVE IS

after Billie Holiday

Unless you learn
The context
Mondrian's *Broadway Boogie-Woogie*
A gridwork of red, yellow, blue, black, and white
That amounts to a city
Crowded with solitude

How lips taste
Is the juice of speculation
I guess you
Flipped your heart and lost
Without a single
Thought of reminiscing

Red square, black square
Of Malevich, the very measure
Of space, white
A wall of ambient sound
To the left, people
To the right, none

The taste of tears is salty
The feel of sleepless eyes
Is nowhere
A trumpet solo
Is all you know of
What love is

RENDEZVOUS CHEZ FATIMATA

after Orquesta Aragon

Let's get together tonight
At Fatimata's place
The *son cubano* makes us happy
Now you feel it
The people are dancing
Down thru the years
A mix of *guarachas*
The elegance of style
The sky full of stars
A moonlit night

My heart will never forget
That feeling of happiness

Learn, boy
Climb the scales
Dance on the roof of the world

This music lends dignity to the proceedings
Then explodes in a burst of joy

What are the odds?
Who would have thought?
Is there a parallel universe
Where all the same things happen?

I'm not going off the deep end
The rhythm of life continues

Mountains of eventuality
Stand out against a violet sky

BOLEROS PSICODÉLICOS

after Adrian Quesada

She enters to a seductive beat
Stirring potentiality
She wants it all
The ocean, the sky above
The dry sun
Laughter like a motorcycle going away
You didn't tell me
What you like
To spend time before it slips off
As the ultimate girl would have it

Where are you?
Where are you going
With your love?
Say no more of
The solitude of your torments
Under the sun
You care only for adventure
Do not forget me
The drums signal from afar
Thoughts of you surround me

This longing
Is it slavery or love?
These lips
Want only
The universe
If only
You would accept the truth

The boy with sad eyes
Has been trying to tell you
On the water's edge

This sleepy fishing village
Ends in a beach
Cloaked in bougainvillea
Under a clear blue sky
This is where I see you
Coming toward me
Please continue your footsteps
Right on up to my door
My house is your house
Now and forever

The longing you mention
Is a way of resetting time
To match the inner resources of this love
That creeps and slithers into the shade
The noon sun casts on the street
She exits through that door
Her mind is made up
Of collective memories
Of Japan, Malaysia, Colombia, France
Places you can only imagine

CELLO SUITES

after Bach and Pablo Casals

Legend has it
He found the scores
At age 13
In a second-hand shop
In Barcelona
Practiced for ten years
Before the first public performance
In 1901

He made his first recordings at Abbey Road studios
    in 1936
He finished in 1950

"I was obliged to be industrious"
Bach had said
"Whoever is equally industrious
Will succeed equally well"

"How could anyone think of Bach as cold?"
Casals remarked
"When these suites shine
With the most glittering kind of poetry"

Bach left no "indications"
Of tempo, dynamics, bowing, styles of play,
    and various curlicues

If nothing else
The lack of a manuscript in Bach's hand
Has ruled out any definitive claims of authenticity

MABANZO

after Juanita Euka

When you write about rain
Don't forget about the tears
You shed on the riverbank
Or when moving between sound and bay
The water moves fast through the channel
Memories heap up
Light on water releases the spirit
Words slip the mind
Like the loss of proper names

I would have given you the earth
A walk on the word side
We deploy the vocabulary
Of an aging planet
The people move from south to north
Chord progressions in their wake
Time to take stock
Awareness of compression
The soul of Africa
From where we started

Even though we have no words
For what is happening
We cling to the earth's surface
Consisting mainly of water
That moves with the mind
Under the sun
Stretching across galaxies
Laughing between waves

Breaking the silence
Of unpopulated space

The truth is real
Only you can break the chain
To soak your frame
In a bath of recollections
Admitting curlicues of thought
The glory of life
The crux of the matter
Sailing away
Over the tops of tall buildings
The repetitions of the heart

SONG FOR MY FATHER

after Horace Silver

Not all people have fathers
There are lots of different ways to make a baby
Many different ways to grow up
Different people who can make a family
My dad was always there for me

In his boyhood on the farm
The whole family slept out on a porch
Mother, father, and three sons
A one-room schoolhouse
A love of reading

The Depression
The move to Tennessee
The University
The trombone
Harvard

WWII
England
My mom
Evanston
Me

With my parents at the Shattuck Hotel
Standing in line for registration
Horace Silver is just in front of us
Unabashed, I welcome Horace to the Bay Area
Knowing that he's come for a gig

He is cordial and polite
I introduce him to my father
Later when Dad is in hospital
I bring a cassette of Horace's trio sides
The music brings us comfort

My father drove me to high school every morning
On his way to the University of Cincinnati
Where he taught English lit

At a state park in Indiana
He kept Nick and me in stitches
With his improvisational wit

As a kid on the beach at Northwestern
I loved to swim between his legs
And climb up on his back

He was always there, and he still is

RED PLANET

after Eric Dolphy

Restless seas under pale night skies
Oh numerous, haphazard and light
When standing in the rain
Of another planet
We pick up signals
That herald new forms of life
They somersault into view

When in the early moments
Of an extended search
We crack open the windows
Test all the doors
Before hurtling into space
An unsuspected place
The charismatic domain of the new

A cartoon character
Avec hat and beard
Arrives in a rush
To take down the minutes
Detail the proceedings
Capture the essence
Leaves town without a trace

A patchwork of countryside
Scotch broom and sea rose
Something sweet
Something tender

Everything evident
Alive in the hills
Alone in June

CHIMURENGA REBEL

after Thomas Mapfumo

Everything that happens
Happens millions of times
As your time and my time
Are entirely different
Yet one in the same

The line curves with the earth
A coat of many colors
Clinging to a rock
Hurtling through space
The straight line too is circular

The return of the chorus
Anchors us in this space
A groove at one with time
Where we can be together
In the river's flow

Carried along by the current
The current battle for liberation
That is our life on earth
Is framed in the small actions
Of the everyday

A phone call from the beyond
A dream of a tall stranger
Walking alone in a town
Seashells in a coastal road
Distant music

Let the dancers have the floor
They know how to use it
The sky is a tent
A big tent of clouds
To shade the dancers

ESTE ES NUESTRO CHANGÜÍ

after Changüí de Guantánamo

This road we are going on
Stretches out in advance of our going
Of hills and waters
It is the very knowledgeable guide
We stop only to go hard
Into the starry night
To the lady of our midnight hour
The child of our morning
The man of noon
This road, this road

Skin of our skin
Sliding down the scale
From rich to poor in a day
Abandoned to dreams at night
We move against the times
Absorb the taste of flames
Stoop to enter the door
Sit among revelers
March with the masses
Happy to be with the people

The call of the instruments
Is heard in the air
A joyful sound
From somewhere over there
The neighbor must be sawing
Or turning on the tap

We live in the busy city
The density's over the top
Whenever you get here
We will be glad to see you

THE MANDÉ VARIATIONS

after Toumani Diabaté

Bass, melody, and improvisation
A single player plays all three
Simultaneously
On the 21-string *kora*
A *griot*
Who can trace his family back 71 generations
To when the Mandé Empire
Controlled much of West Africa
The music is contemplative, spiritual, delightful
Fit for meditation, driving, and massage

The interplay of theme and variation
Weaves a net of responses
Memories, dreams, and reflections
Life a string of repetitions
Singular episodes rise up
Out of the epicenter of September
A concatenation of centuries

These songs bring with them
The life of the people
Stitched into scales and runs
Harmony a steady hand on the tiller
As a boat glides over ocean depths
Populated by sea life for eons
Songs of conflict, exile, and return

What adventures await us in the cave of tomorrow?
What peaks to climb?

What thriving cities to explore?
The lights of family fires glow bright
In desert night
Wholly undiscoverable by morning
A cool bath in a perfect oasis

Don't try to play my style
You play your style
I play my style
Together we make a new style
That is the secret of world music
The secret of world peace is big love

Tens

I–LXXIII

2 January–17 November 2023

I

Back to here
Where what is *is*
Is what?
You make it up
The rain clouds hanging
Heavy overhead
The list of things to do
Short
The year ahead
Wide open

II

Rain today
An atmospheric bomb
We wait for
In suspended animation
Winds at 22 mph
A letter is a bridge
Between friends
A construct of words
In the form of raindrops
Beading up on a windowpane

III

To write like a mad one
One must write every day
Day in and day out
Out of sheer desire
Desire with no object
Objects are overrated
Over the long haul
Haul away these broke-ass signs
These memories piling up
Up in the ozone layer

IV

Those white dots floating randomly about
Under a steel-gray sky
Heavy with impending rain
Turn out to be seagulls wheeling offshore
Then wham! It hits, a sudden shower
Mixed pinpoints of rain and hail
Smash rooftops, strike timpani
Against windows, bear down on
The street, now here, now gone
The story of a life in miniature

V

Wild wicked wind
Blows trees around without
Lifting them off the ground
Sleeping bag flops across Lakeshore
All types of people
What were their names?
The wind picks them up
Puts them down someplace different
Sweeps plum blossoms off the patio
Into piles like snowdrifts

VI

You write yourself out of a paper bag
Every time you play on your instrument
With both hands
What's going on
Is walking and talking
By dint of foot and word of mouth
82 percent of Americans don't go nowhere
The trees go wild in the wind
The clouds open up into a downpour
And *that's* what's going on in this neck of the woods

VII

Motor sounds smooth the surface of the lagoon
Pelicans soar, glide, dive, disperse
Return to float, beat wings, splash off
Dull fog canopy overhead
Man looks at watch
Selects an oar, drops board into water
Pushes off
Returns to dock
Chooses different board
Paddles out, disappears from view

VIII

The river is over there
West northwest from here
At the airport hotel
Where we must stay
Our flight canceled
Due to severe flooding
To the east
We will try again
Tomorrow morning
The sky gods permitting

IX

Music is all about scheduling
The calendar a complex instrument
With 365 keys
Times a hundred years of solitude
Which is practice
You practice every time you play
The need for subs is satisfied
By the community at large
Someone will jump at the chance
The energy flows through gateless barriers

X

Just before rehearsal
Charged up on anticipation
The host musician prepares the way
Plugs in the devices
Makes sure everything works
Perfection is always out of reach
But the effort to get there
Leads to something else
Unanticipated conglomerate of the group setting
Alive in the moment

XI

A new day dawns in all its brightness
A tube stop in London town
Up in the morning and off to school
The school of hard knocks
That knock your socks off
You are caught red headed
Attending to something or other
The main thing escapes your notice
Because it is always on
The life force building up steam

XII

Starting from sleep
The engine of last night's dream
Purrs over beaches, mountains, monasteries
The natural world of relations
Drum to voice to flute
A long tone in an open field
Meanwhile rumors of war
Prolong like melancholy
Dozing under certain grief
Much to the profit in arms

XIII

Somewhere between the first and third person
A tight end catches a long pass
Later breaks through the line
Makes family proud
A lifetime of injuries
Adds up to one
I ain't got to worry
'Cause my work is done
See you later, alligator
Bust your chops on peppermint candy

XIV

Nothing is the same to more than one person
There is no single face in nature
Every eye sees from its own angle
For the night has a thousand eyes
And a thousand eyes can't help but see
There are more things in heaven and earth
Than are dreamed of in your philosophy
Every man's spice-box seasons his own food
I pick up reflections of the life around me
And absorb them according to my inside juices

XV

The conference closes with a couple of keynotes
Two gel caps, one black, one brown
The dream specifies its reversible contents
One hard-core serious, the other more humorous
More humane you might say
I say this in broad daylight
An arpeggiated tree trunk
Reaches for the sky
To the tune of Nocturne No. 2, Op. 9
As recorded by Vladimir Sofronitsky in 1949

XVI

Nothing between names and pictures
The gaps are filled with feeling
A feeling for leaving
Little to go on and well enough to leave alone
A visitor from space
Dropped down into flickering time
Determined to find a sub
As the music must go on
The living require it
In the form of a thousand dances

XVII

I won't have this kind of time again for a while
Considering the minerality of bath salts
There will be tacos, so bring your appetite
Lunch on the calendar of dreams
The white spaces burn in broad daylight
A one-person percussion section
Arrives at a point of departure
Easily slips into another world
Composed of figments
The true test of a sound engineer

XVIII

Whether to send tanks
Or push for a cease-fire
This was the bone of contention
In the Ginsberg home pre-WWII
Communist Naomi called for intervention
Socialist Louis argued restraint
Young Allen favored war on fascism
Later vowing to save all beings
Chanting *om* in the face of tear gas
As demonstrators stream through the gates

XIX

Colossal, sculpted heads
Carved from tons of basalt
Represent Olmec leaders
Wearing the leather helmets of ball players
An inscribed staircase built at Yaxchilán
To honor Bird Jaguar the Great
Who kicks a huge rubber ball
Containing the body of his rival, Jeweled Skull
The central feature of a carved lintel
On a nearby temple

XX

Wars are "contests of injury"
Anyone killed or disfigured remains so
Even if largely theatrical
As in Homeric-style warfare
Where heroes taunted, jeered, and occasionally
Threw javelins or shot arrows at one another
Sovereignty, bureaucracy, and politics
Types of domination grounded respectively
In the use of violence, knowledge, and charisma
Form the three-legged stool of the state

XXI

Politicians on both sides
Have hoodwinked their people
Now all must suffer
How many people can this world hold
A woman holding a child
A man holding another man in contempt
A child climbing over a pile of rubble
Regional conflict
Rumors of war
Pulse of big city vibration

XXII

Who wreaked havoc on the hospital?
They both did
Impossible to assign blame
In the fog of war
All my ancient car mechanics
Couldn't put the van back on the road
Tone rows file out of the sensorium
To the beat of the timing chain
Diplomacy must play catch-up
To grim truth in the absence of time

XXIII

Back to where
History begins
News of warring tribes
Overlapping demographics
Conflicting reports
The wave of the future
Mixed blood harmonics
Up the neck of the bass
All beings safe
All beings free

XXIV

Off the coast of France near Cherbourg
In an important battle of the American Civil War
The U.S.S. Kearsarge attacked and sank
The Confederate boat the C.S.S. Alabama
On June 19, 1864, an event depicted
By Edouard Manet in his first known seascape
And first painting of a current event
The picture was displayed in the window
Of Alfred Cadart's print shop in Paris
Barely a month after the incident took place

XXV

Staring off into space
Resting head in hand
Ignoring her brandy-soaked plum and unlit cigarette
She gazes wistfully into the distance
The black dots of her pupils
Calibrate the balance of inside and out
Time stands still
The pink of her attire
Continuous under the pale marble tabletop
The picture frame on the wall behind her is repeated
    in the frame of this picture

XXVI

The space between days
The day the earth stood still
Channel switching
Night of the living dead
The space between life and death
Between words and things
The spaces between people
Between things to do on Mars
Between language, thought, and reality
The spaces between peoples

XXVII

Like water
On two sides of a dam
What separates the ordinary
From the radiant
Is the curtain of the ego
Remove said separation
It all flows together
Now we're going to tear down
The iron gate
And let those fish run through

XXVIII

While hacking around in the attic
The thought occurred to me
That meaning is neither several nor level
Rather it is distributed
Across time and place
Different by day
A slow train of particles
Arriving from all directions
Sequential, indigenous, and round
About a world in diameter

XXIX

Anything can happen anytime
You could wind up dead
Who left a note on the roof of the back house?
How I became a political operative
It was my idea to flipflop the campaign managers
Sometimes Democrats look more like Republicans
The sun put in an appearance
The day dressed in chill splendor
That long walk will have to wait
How do you like your coffee?

XXX

The lights go out
All over town
A shadow moves
Across a face
A *noir* moment
On a blank page
What will you give me
For this marvelous art?
Do I hear money?
Or only see the change?

XXXI

Stars in winter
Palpable shine
To forget is a blessing
Leaves the soul free
Like an exchange student in Bosnia
Doing shots in a club
An end to specificity
A crystal set
Far out to sea
Traffic in sound

XXXII

Time for a smoke
A non-filter stashed away
A step away from them
The family of choice
Hop on a bike
Head for the hills
Off-road green and rolling hills
That repeat along a coastline
The return is all uphill
And absolutely worth the effort

XXXIII

I think therefore I am
I think therefore of others
I is another and so is you
We reverberate in a group orchestration of otherness
That sounds like something else
Including plants, animals, rivers, and mountains
Languages, regions, nights, and days
Is another way to put it
At home in the cosmos

XXXIV

Seize on these moments (lying in wait)
And throw them away
The life you lived is over now
That bird has flown
Shelves of books of accretive sensitivity
Porous pages of paper marking time
Off you go
You or I or they or we
Making of air our permanent home
Unpacking a life like no other

XXXV

Sensitive arms and legs
Fall outside the scope
Of recent memory
Blurred by the news
Of having to be moved
Something one never wanted
Who was adamant in their autonomy
And didn't know what was going on
The daughter as yet uninformed
The truth hiding in plain sight

XXXVI

I guess I'll just pass through life
Like a walk on San Pablo Avenue
In springtime when the sky is bright
With availability
Our vocabulary directs our movements
The movies stored in our heads
The past perfect on the cutting room floor
A soloistic aside
Going to the store for supplies
What happens was going to

XXXVII

Goods and services
No self without an other
Shiny surfaces
Away with nervousness
Take it like a mother
No walk in the park
When on we go
On the count of one
One tangled afternoon
In Tokyo

XXXVIII

The mind/body extends from the earth's core
To stars fleeing each other at the speed of light
In a time of destitution, it resembles an empty husk
Other times if fills with impressions, colors, sounds,
    tastes, delights
Who is this one who has braved the passages of time
Who stands before you open mouth to speak
Then slips into the shadow of a doubt
The sun breaks up into a river of gold
Then cascades down through a landscape
Of darker and darker matter

XXXIX

Extra! Extra! Read all about it!
A coolness settles under the trees
The earth rocks us in its cradle
We live amid linguistic noise
Cosmic hubbub of factory, of market
While icecaps, while seas grow historic
What happens today stays fresh
Men, women read time like a book
Jet noise our very nature
Climbing back out of the buzz

XL

It must be fast as life is fast
The connecting passage is lost
Gravity gives us the vertical
As morning light through orange curtains hangs
"Mister President, with great respect I must tell you
That in the long history of the world
This is a thing to do now"
A grey wind stirs ancient trees
Reflectographs capture the light
A bird sings their particular song

XLI

Undrafted players score 56 points for the Heat
The wind has a tang to it
Waves break on rocks along the shoreline
We hang from the cliff of the line into empty space
Breathe into the gap
The rising sun brings light back into the room
At day's end, a skeletal pier
Where men compete for the ghost of a dance
Writing letters in water to one another
As distance makes the heart grow stronger

XLII

But wait, there's more!
This is a big, beautiful universe we live in
That's been given to us
And here's an example of just how magnificent and
encompassing it is
Terns circle and dive where the fish are
We chase them trailing lures from two rods
The sky dissolves into bands of yellow, orange, rose,
violet, grey, blue
The single dot of a lighthouse on a dark spit
No man is a long skinny island
The secret of life is enjoying the passage of time

XLIII

Overturn the stability of fixed ideas
The mind is a flashing apparatus
Quick to scan a room
Interrupted conversation on phone with skull
Directing a team of short-long arms and legs
Beware of banners occulting the right of way
The alternating glories of day and night
We are individuals in a group shot
The white race is overrated
The color of blood is red

XLIV

The pronoun *they* is a natural way to tag the non-
    binary individual
Awkward at first, with an effort of concentration
It can become second nature
But there is another benefit lurking under the surface
The third-person plural also explodes the unitary
    representation of the individual subject
We are composite
Each one comprises multiple persons
Your sister, your brother, your mother, your father, your
    grandparents, your teachers, your ancestors,
    your friends
When we invite you over
Who will walk through that door?

XLV

I didn't know that bird lime
Concretizes itself in the form of a perfect ash
On a bluestone table in late spring
By combining sweet and dry vermouth with bourbon
   and bitters
Sheila fashions a Perfect Manhattan
No single model remembered as ideal
Can integrate all the contemporary complexities
Of diverse and dynamic individual psyches
Defended group identities, huge populations
And multiple ways that people look at and are
   constituted by their surroundings

XLVI

Green, green old rocky road
Promenading for nautical miles
Reading back the minutes from a meeting
    of the minds
A photo of the dualists with their seconds
Every day I sing the blues
Churchill hated to hear a man whistle
The sound of the diaphone is heard along the shore
The boats barely visible after dark
I can only tell you what's happening in my sector
The experience is obscured by its description

XLVII

Non-dangerous wrecks cast aeronautical light
Underwater cities destroyed, to be reestablished
Lights are white unless otherwise indicated
What one can do one must do
Or take up vows and live as a nun
Perhaps to spar with one's better angels
Until a reflector lights up a path through the darkness
Where a temporary buoy bobs
Beyond the white hull of a fishing boat
Under a sky of violet, pink, yellow, and orange

XLVIII

Red clay cliffs plunge down into the Sound
Coral shoals structure undersea narratives of
    crustacean significance
Like wheels on a gravel road
A memory the smell of cut grass
And here we are stuck in the mud
Between a rock and a hard-to-place face
Unfolding our chairs at a spot on the sand
A patio of broken shells at the seafood shack
A history of the cinema in black and white
When we get back our host is lost in a brown study

XLIX

I sit back and sink into the sensorium
The color of water is jello
I address my claim to the Bureau of Engraving
    and Printing
Mutilated Currency Division, Room 344-A
And affix a self-canceling stamp
Why wait when the future is only the illusion of certain
    images?
It's time to go outside and breathe the air
As always
By placing a lifetime of lunch breaks end to end
We hope to promote absence as our finest
    achievement

L

I sometimes emulate others
In hopes of being as unlike myself as I can be
My writing involves continuous displacements
Of subject positions the very flower
Who put the sin in Sinaloa?
You could offprint the comix with silly putty
The Loop abuts the Lake
The Field Museum, Soldier Field
In a bath of crystal basalt
In a tub of golden pathways

LI

Everything is getting more chaotic
Not just healthcare, but everything
The weather, for example
Mountains of prose collapse
Into rivulets of real time
We try to figure everything out
Before it trickles through our fingers
But it ain't easy making a go of it
Out here in Entropica
The land of what once was

LII

The jingling of keys
From C to B flat
A trailing off
Where the sun goes to die
On Sullivan Street
Where what you get
Is noise plus
The genuine article
Of sleep
In other, better words

LIII

What you said
In the interim
Is juice
To my three-of-a-kind
Make way for the Little King
A cartoon version of oneself
As a small child
If I tell you the chords
Can you wing it?
The weather? It's nice

LIV

While waiting for water to evaporate
How about this one
This one-way ticket to who knows where
A morning as wrapped in mystery
As it is cloaked in desire
Where potential builds momentum
Out of feathers and twigs
To raise a conference of birds
Alighting on the neighborhood
Before pulling out entirely

LV

The idea of writing and writing are not the same
The idea of a river and a river are totally different
A river requires tributaries and a mouth
An idea needs someone to occur to
The mouth is speaking but it's only words
If I could, I would sing you a melody so mild
How many different kinds of bird have occupied these
trees?
The idea of a poem and a poem are next door
neighbors
There is no such thing as silence
Someone or something is always making a sound

LVI

I write to find out what I have to say
Whether I agree with it or not
It's your move
Whether you like it or not
Our relative pronouns are old friends
Lounging around in the turf
Like a horseless carriage
Seen through a tan barn door
They finish each other's sentences
And dot each other's i's

LVII

I shing my ostracization
The boss tells the boss: boss
Was there life before life?
If they push that button, kiss your ass goodbye
My present activities may be seen in the old light of
  my accoutrements
I have been over-exposed all my life
Dancing, like kosher ice water
Imagine throwing away the avalanche so early in
  the movie
Opprobrious shrilling
Time, progress and good sense

LVIII

Poetry is an inside job
Committed by someone with first-hand knowledge of
 the business
A critic chronicles the caper
The way an author drops clues
Gradually and with time off for behavior
The metaphor is generally mixed
Spinning at flash points where meanings coincide
The sky is like a sail
Spread out over a crowd of people
Who hurry on with their busy lives

LIX

This is a hotel now
It used to be a gas station
The streets are dark, the traffic, light
The weather, mild
The music, out of sight
When such as we
Are bound to flee
The moment
Seat of unbelievable angst
Take refuge in the beckoning tides

LX

This paroxysm of sound and dappled light
Is when and where we live
A series of shocks that pile up
In time to constitute our system
A vast machine with ideas of its own
Of which we are the argument
We open one door after another
The yellow, the purple, the white, the green
Each room a monochrome understanding
The red and the black, the quick and the dead

LXI

I see little point
In the things I do
I detach and float
Somewhere out of reach
Of signification
Where voices are shadows
Of disbelief
I circulate
A shark in a tank
A letter enclosed in a word

LXII

Wrap your senses around the scaffolding of
    the century
A century is more than enough time to expect to live
Time has a way of opening up or snapping shut
In memory, it is a montage of images
Loosely associated or collapsing one into the next
In anticipation, it is a fantasy formed of fragments of
    past lives
Since we cannot accurately imagine the future
To do so is the work of the visionary lying on a sofa
You who have been here since the breakfast of time
Remember that walk in the park and the bed that
    came out from the wall?

LXIII

It's a question of scale
Two nearly identical persons
Male or female? I can't tell
Walk by the school
Both in khaki pants, white jackets, white caps
They walk in perfect, unconscious lockstep
What is the meaning of this?
I ask from the bedroom window
The voice of Philip Whalen
An echo in my head

LXIV

Surf pounds the shore on the mysterious island
Chichén Itzá stands alone in time
Some facts are nothing but distant cousins
I once was lost but now I'm found
Repeat after me
Red leather, yellow leather, red leather, yellow leather
Old Tolstoy's cow, old Tolstoy's cow
Such tongue-twisters are key to the actor's training
Correct me if I'm wrong
"Carry me back to Old Virginny"

LXV

Before is after and after is before
Time does a somersault
Old New York is now new
A bearded guy in a Yankees cap pushing a broom
Time to bring coffee up to our room
While bass thunders out through the lobby
Thin blonde Lesbian athletes all in black
Descend a staircase
Fire in place of screenage
Take the long way around

LXVI

In memory of Susan Hopkins Coolidge
(1943-2023)

She went so fast
And now she's gone
Gone in a flash
Is how they put it
We put it down
To impermanence
But how can one
So crucial to what's going on
Be so fully present
And then so suddenly not?

LXVII

In memory of Clairmont Moore (1939-2023)

You are white, he said
I am black
But we can talk
After all the food he cooked
Many bottles of wine
Weed from the lady's son
Much hilarity
Sitting on his balcony
Our friendship spanning years
Talk jumping the gap

LXVIII

Is it simple sentence or simple syrup?
An indivisible station for controlling flights
Passengers are dandified in their noisy semblance
A thumping floor that motivates the action
Who else but we in the autumn of the night
Characters on street corners walking away
Home to bed is the order of the hour
A slippery syntax that clicks back together when you
    aren't looking
Suddenly bright when half empty
Partially close to true

LXIX

Incident brain-flash report
Walking down Washington Avenue
Form is emptiness
Emptiness is form
An equal sign is a landscape
Horizon of sea and sky
Without a net
Haiku crouching under a bridge
Memorializing the time
Meanwhile, and there usually is one

LXX

Much to say
More to write
Still more to keep in the head
That bank of sites
To be realized
At some later date
Always accumulate
Never retreat
On we go
Who carry you hence

LXXI

The past weighs like an Alp
On the brain of the living
I rifle through a dense fog of memories
Toss and turn to reenter sleep
In anticipation of daylight
Butter, eggs, arborio rice, bow tie pasta, garbanzos
A long line leading to a black mountain
A white ladder all covered in water
Throw it away
Walk like an Egyptian

LXXII

Being with fire
Being with water
Being with trees
Standing still
For long periods of time
Try to forget who you were
By the end of the long sit
Wandering through worlds
Too many to count
Water collects in beads on leaves

LXXIII

Now they tell me identity is a construction site
I'll have water neat and a side of bricks
Now they tell me memory is porous
A memory like a sieve
The foreign legion is in town
Batten down the hatches
Smoke 'em if you got 'em
Traffic in goods, hoards of the bad
The last time I was here I nearly died laughing
Remember me to your extended family

Notes for *Tens*

V. "What were their names": Woody Guthrie, "The Sinking of the Reuben James" (1942)

IX. "You practice every time you play": Thelonious Monk in documentary film *Straight No Chaser* (1988) directed by Charlotte Zwerin; line 10: *Wumen Huikai, The Gateless Barrier: The Wu-Men Kuan (Mumonkan)* (1228), translated by Robert Aitkin (1991)

XII. line 9: Peter Tosh, song, "Rumors of War" on album, *Mystic Man* (1979); Matthew 24:6–13–"You will hear of wars and rumors of wars but see that you are not alarmed. Such things must happen, but the end is still to come."

XIII. "I ain't got to worry": Tom Verlaine, Television, song, "Glory," album, *Adventure* (1978); "Bust your chops on peppermint candy," Stuff Smith, song, "If You're a Viper" (1936); Alex Chilton, song, "You's a Viper," album, *Set* (2017)

XIV. "Nothing is the same … no single face in nature … I pick up reflections … inside juices," Zora Neal Hurston, *Dust Tracks on a Road* (1942)

XV. lines 9-10: Frederic Chopin, Nocturne in E Flat Major (1932)

XVI. line 3: Ted Berrigan, *A Feeling for Leaving* (1975)

XVII. line 8: Henry Threadgill, album, *Easily Slip into Another World* (1987); Henry Threadgill and Brent Hayes Edwards, book, *Easily Slip into Another World: A Life in Music* (2023)

XVIII. lines 1-10: Michael Schumacher, *Dharma Lion: The Life of Allen Ginsberg* (1992)

XIX. lines 1-10: David Graeber and David Wengrow, *The Dawn of Everything: A New History of Humanity* (2021)

XX. lines 1-10: David Graeber and David Wengrow, op. cit.

XXII. line 4: James G. Blight and Janet M. Lang, *The Fog of War: Lessons from the Life of Robert S. McNamara* (1985); *The Fog of War: 11 Lessons from the Life of Robert S. McNamara*, documentary film directed by Errol Morris (2003): line 5: "All my ancient, twisted karma / from beginningless greed, hate, and delusion, / born though body, speech, and mind / I now fully avow." Repentance chant, Zen Buddhism; line 8: Douglas Woolf, *The Timing Chain*, novel (1985).

XXIII. line 3: J.H. Prynne, *News of Warring Clans* (1977); lines 9-10: Hozan Alan Senauke, "Witness to a Nightmare in Israel and Gaza," email, October 2023: "May all beings be safe; may all beings be free."

XXIV. lines 1-10: Edouard Manet, *The Battle of the USS Kearsarge and the C.S.S. Alabama* (1864)

XXV. lines 1-10: Edouard Manet, *Plum Brandy*, (ca. 1877)

XXVII. "Like water … all flows together," Sojun Mel Weitsman, *Seeing One Thing Through: The Zen Life and Teachings of Sojun Mel Weitsman* (2023); "Now we're going to tear down / The iron gate / And let those fish run through," Peter Brucker, "Tear Down the Iron Gate," SoundCloud (2022)

XXXIII. line 8: Alfred Bester, *The Stars My Destination* (1957)

XL. lines 5-7: Winston Churchill to Franklin Delano Roosevelt, as quoted in *The Splendid and the Vile: A Saga of Churchill, Family, and Defiance During the Blitz* by Erik Larson (2020); line 9: Reflectographs are cameraless photographs made by a point of light reflected onto photosensitive paper, the brainchild of scientist, naturalist, printer, inventor, and photographer Alan W. Bernheimer (1913-2006).

XLI. line 7: Frances Richard, *Gordon Matta-Clark: Physical Poetics* (2019); David Hammons, *Day's End*, Whitney Museum of American Art, Hudson River Park (2021); line 9: Inscription on the gravestone of John Keats: "*Here lies One Whose Name was writ in Water. 24 February 1821.*"

XLII. "This is a big, beautiful universe … encompassing it is," John Coltrane interview, *Downbeat* (April 12, 1962); line 9: John Donne, "No Man Is an Island" in *Devotions upon Emergent Occasions* (1624); "The secret of life is enjoying the passage of time," James Taylor, bench inscription at Gay Head Lighthouse, Martha's Vineyard

XLV. "No single model … constituted by their surroundings," James Sherry, *Selfie: Poetry, Social Change and Ecological Connection* (2022)

XLVI. line 1: Dave Van Ronk, song, "Green, Green Old Rocky Road"(1963)

LXVIII. line 3: Lucinda Williams, album, *Car Wheels on a Gravel Road* (1998)

LI. line 9: Kit Robinson, prose poem, "Entropica," *Down and Back* (1978)

LIII. line 5: *The Little King*, gag-a-day comic strip by Otto Soglow (1930-1975)

LIV. line 8: "The Conference of the Birds," Persian poem by Sufi poet Farid al-din Attar, commonly known as Attar of Nishapur (1177); *Conference of the Birds*, album by bassist Dave Holland with tenor saxophonist Sam Rivers, alto saxophonist Anthony Braxton and percussionist Barry Altschul (1973); radio show hosted by Stephen Cope, WRFI Community Radio, www.wrfi.org

LV. line 9: John Cage, commenting on the first performance of his silent composition *4'33"* (1952)

LVII. lines 1-10: Drew Gardner, editor, *Ingenious Pleasures: An Anthology of Punk, Trash and Camp in 20th Century Poetry* (2023), lines quoted from poems by Abraham Lincoln Gillespie, Tristan Tzara, Bern Porter, Sun Ra, Jackson Mac Low, Taylor Mead, Kenneth Koch, Frank O'Hara, Russell Atkins, and John Ashbery

LX. "We open one door … a monochrome understanding," Roger Corman, director, *House of Usher* (1960), based on "The Fall of the House of Usher" by Edgar Allen Poe (1839); line 10: Stendhal, *Le Rouge et le Noir* (1830); Sam Raimi, director, *The Quick and the Dead* (1995)

LXIV. line 1: Jules Verne, *The Mysterious Island* (1875); line 4: John Newton, "Amazing Grace," Christian hymn (1779); lines 5-8: Actor's training exercise led by Nick Robinson in production of *Particle Arms* by Alan Bernheimer, Poets Theater, San Francisco (1982); line 10: James L. Bland, "Carry Me Back to Old Virginny" (1878)

LXIX. "Walking down Washington Avenue," Robert Grenier, *CAMBRIDGE M'ASS*; poster (1979); "Form is emptiness/Emptiness is form," *The Heart Sutra*, classic text of Mahayana Buddhism (661); *Without a Net*, live album by Wayne Shorter Quartet (2013)

LXX. "Much to say … keep in the head," Arkadii Dragomoshchenko, postcard to KR (Bancroft Library, University of California, Berkeley)

LXXI. lines 1-2: Karl Marx, "The Eighteenth Brumaire of Louis Napoleon" (1852): "The tradition of all dead generations weighs like an Alp on the brains of the living;" 'A white ladder all covered in water,' Bob Dylan, "A Hard Rain's A-Gonna Fall," *The Freewheelin' Bob Dylan*, album (1963); "Throw it away," Ludwig Wittgenstein, *Tractatus Logico-Philosophicus*, 6.54 (1962): "My propositions serve as elucidations in the following way: anyone who understands me eventually recognizes them as nonsensical, when he has used them—as steps—to climb beyond them. (He must, so to speak, throw away the ladder after he has climbed up it)…"; line 10: The Bangles, *Walk Like an Egyptian*, album (1986)

LXXII. lines 1-5: Kit Robinson, "Ice Cubes II," *Balance Sheet* (1993); lines 6-7: *Bowed Some, Chanted a Little: Philip Whalen's Zen Journals and the San Francisco Renaissance*, ed. Brian Unger (2023); line 10: Robinson, op. cit.

LXXIII, line 4: Kit Robinson, "The Sieve," *The Crave* (2002)